W9-CKL-446

Virtual Apprentice

CARTOON ANIMATOR

By Don Rauf
and Monique Vescia

Ferguson

An imprint of Infobase Publishing

Virtual Apprentice: Cartoon Animator

Ferguson
An imprint of Infobase Publishing
132 West 31st Street
New York, NY 10001

Library of Congress Cataloging-in-Publication Data

Rauf, Don.
  Virtual apprentice. Cartoon animator / Don Rauf and Monique Vescia.
    p. cm.
  Includes bibliographical references and index.
  ISBN-13: 978-0-8160-6760-2
  ISBN-10: 0-8160-6760-0
  1. Animated films–Vocational guidance–Juvenile literature. 2.
Animators–Juvenile literature. I. Vescia, Monique. II. Title. III.
Title: Cartoon animator.
  NC1765.R38 2007
  791.43'34023–dc22

                    2007005118

Ferguson books are available at special discounts when purchased in bulk quantities for businesses, associations, institutions, or sales promotions. Please call our Special Sales Department in New York at (212) 967-8800 or (800) 322-8755.

You can find Ferguson on the World Wide Web at http://www.fergpubco.com

Produced by Bright Futures Press (http://www.brightfuturespress.com)
Series created by Diane Lindsey Reeves
Interior design by Tom Carling, carlingdesign.com
Cover design by Salvatore Luongo

Photo List: Table of Contents PACHA/CORBIS; Page 5 Auslöser/zefa/CORBIS; Page 7 Paramount Pictures/Bureau L.A. Collections/ CORBIS; Page 10 Bettmann/CORBIS; Page 19 PACHA/CORBIS; Page 21 Bob Rowan/Progressive Image/CORBIS; Page 25 Belinksy Yuri/ITARTASS/CORBIS; Page 27 CORBIS SYGMA; Page 33 Bob Rowan/Progressive Image/CORBIS; Page 36 Chuck Savage/CORBIS.

Note to Readers: Please note that every effort was made to include accurate Web site addresses for kid-friendly resources listed throughout this book. However, Web site content and addresses change often and the author and publisher of this book cannot be held accountable for any inappropriate material that may appear on these Web sites. In the interest of keeping your on-line exploration safe and appropriate, we strongly suggest that all Internet searches be conducted under the supervision of a parent or other trusted adult.

Printed in the United States of America

BANG BFP 10 9 8 7 6 5 4 3 2 1

This book is printed on acid-free paper.

CONTENTS

The Wonderful World of Animation

American children growing up in the 1960s through the 1990s enjoyed a special weekly ritual: Saturday morning cartoons. Kids would shovel down their Lucky Charms and gather around the tube to watch shows like the *Flintstones* and *Scooby-Doo*. They laughed at animated characters such as a tiny superhero named Mighty Mouse, a slow-witted kid called Fat Albert, a flying squirrel named Rocky, and a moose named Bullwinkle. They could hardly wait for Saturday, when they could see their favorite programs again for one magical morning of the week.

You live in a different world—where entire channels like Nickelodeon and the Cartoon Network broadcast both new and classic animated shows 24/7. It may be hard to picture a TV universe that isn't teeming with cartoons. Any channel-surfer can tell you that lots of the most popular shows on TV today are animated: *SpongeBob SquarePants, South Park, Powerpuff Girls*, and of course *The Simpsons*—the longest running sitcom in American history. Animation is not just for kids anymore—plenty of adults are hooked on these shows, too. Many of the commercials playing on TV today also depend on animation for their special effects.

And that's just the scene on the small screen. Full-length animated pictures are regularly released in theaters across the country. From its humble beginnings at the start of the twentieth century, the art of animation (and the related field of special effects) has exploded into a huge global industry that's projected to earn $100 billion by 2008.

In *Virtual Apprentice: Cartoon Animator*, you'll meet the industry pioneers and the artists who make the magic of animation happen. You'll sneak a peek behind the scenes at an animation studio and learn the secrets and tools of the trade. Join us on a journey from one mouse (named Mickey) to another–the kind that you click, and find out about the latest technologies and trends in this exciting field. Try your hand at some animation techniques, and see if you've got what it takes to join the ranks of these talented and imaginative artists.

Will kids in the future be watching cartoons you created?

The Dawn of Animation

The term *animation* comes from *anima*, a Latin word that means "soul" or "the breath of life." And that's what an animator does—he or she breathes life into two-dimensional characters and gives them heart and soul and personality. Artists working with pencil and sketchpad or a computer mouse create characters that pick themselves up and walk off the page...and sometimes straight over a cliff! Animation has prehistoric beginnings, when early artists tried to capture the animals they saw not just with nets and spears but with images, too. One painted a wild boar with four extra legs, to make it look like it was running. Ancient cave artists wrestled with the same problem that still confronts animators today: How do you create the illusion of motion using still pictures? Part of the solution to this problem has to do with a "flaw" in the human eye.

A Trick of the Eye

"Persistence of vision" may sound like the title of a movie that your dad just rented from Netflix, but it's actually the name of the phenomenon that makes animation possible. Here's how it works: The retina of your eye retains an image it has seen

> "I only hope that we don't lose sight of one thing—that it was all started by a mouse."
>
> —WALT DISNEY, PIONEERING ANIMATOR

Lights! Camera! Action! On the set of *SpongeBob SquarePants*.

for a moment (one-tenth of a second, to be exact) before processing another image. That's why when you swing a glow stick around in the dark, it looks like a solid circle of light. If a series of images are flashed before your eye at 10 frames per second, your brain thinks it sees a single moving image. In the mid-19th century, people began dreaming up different ways to exploit this visual phenomenon. Early animation devices such as the phenakistoscope (1833), the zoetrope (1834), and others with equally weird names, created the appearance of movement with a series of still images.

In 1892, a Frenchman named Emile Reynaud produced the very first animated films. Reynaud created his short films by painting directly on long strips of clear plastic and projecting these images with a special machine he called the praxinoscope, which he had patented in 1877. In the United States, a French-Canadian cartoonist named Raoul Barré and his business partner, William Nolan, opened the first animation studio, in New York City, in 1914. They devised a system called a peg board, which is still used in hand-drawn animation today. Holes are punched at the bottom of the transparent sheets, which fit over the pegs on the bar and keep each sheet in place. This invention made it much easier to create steady animation, since each successive image drawn by the animator could be positioned in the same place.

First Steps

You might say that animated characters, like actual animals, evolved from prehistoric creatures—one dinosaur in particular, that is—a diplodocus named Gertie. Windsor McCay was inspired by the dinosaur models in New York City's Museum of Natural History to create an animated short called *Gertie the Dinosaur*. Gertie, who debuted in 1914, was the first animated character with a personality. In McCay's film she strikes funny poses, does a few dance steps, and even sheds some tears.

Many of the earliest animated characters first appeared in newspaper comic strips, such as *Little Nemo in Slumberland* and the *Katzenjammer Kids*. An exception was Otto Messmer's *Felix the Cat*, which began as an animated cartoon and later became a comic strip. Because Felix reappeared in a series of shorts, his personality could develop over time. Felix was the very first real cartoon star and the first character to have merchandise such as toys and handkerchiefs created in his image. Audiences in the 1920s went nuts for this little black cat.

These early animations were silent unless accompanied by live piano music in the theaters where they were shown. But just as silent live-action movies would be replaced by "talkies," animated films would soon feature sound, too.

Moving at the Speed of Life

Film is projected at the rate of 24 frames per second (fps). Early animators soon figured out that they needed to generate a sequence of about 18 images to create one second of seamless motion. (Some images are repeated to fill the 24 frames.) That means it takes a long time to create even a very short film. Do the math: 18 frames x 60 seconds = 1,080 separate frames for one minute of film, and each one was drawn by hand. In 1914, Earl Hurd started inking the animators' drawings onto transparent sheets of celluloid. That way, characters could be moved as necessary, but the background wouldn't have to be retraced for every frame that was filmed. Hurd's invention of "cel animation" was a huge advance in the art form and saved animators a great deal of time. (The term "cel" now means a single painted transparency from an animated film.)

The Man Behind the Mouse

Walt Disney (1901–1966) was born in Chicago, Illinois, at the beginning of the twentieth century. He wasn't an especially

Buddy System

Match the animated character with his or her sidekick.

POP QUIZ

1 Yogi Bear and
  A. Boo-Boo
  B. Baa-Baa
  C. La-La

2 The Tick and
  A. the Tock
  B. Arthur
  C. Beatrice

3 Bart Simpson and
  A. Smithers
  B. Groundskeeper Willie
  C. Milhouse

4 Sonic the Hedgehog and
  A. Snails
  B. Tonic
  C. Tails

5 SpongeBob SquarePants and
  A. Patrick
  B. Squidward
  C. Plankton

6 Ren and
  A. Stimpy
  B. Stumpy
  C. Abercrombie

ANSWERS: 1-A, 2-B, 3-C, 4-C, 5-A, 6-A

Walt Disney (on left) talks to composers about the musical score for *Fantasia*.

good student, but he could draw, and sometimes Walt amused his classmates by sketching little figures in the margins of his books and then flipping the pages to make them move. With his older brother, Roy, Walt started a small animation studio to create short cartoons for various clients. Early on the brothers nearly went broke and had to borrow money from their uncle to keep the business afloat.

In 1923, Disney moved his studio from Kansas City, Missouri, to Hollywood, California. Accompanying Disney westward were Hugh Harman, who went on to found Warner Bros., and Rudy Ising, who started MGM. In time these three studios would become the leaders in the animation industry. Setting up house next to the big-time movie studios in Hollywood was a smart move: By the 1930s and 1940s, animated shorts, including Max Fleischer's Betty Boop cartoons and *Popeye*, were regularly shown in theaters before the feature film.

The House That Walt Built

Walt Disney was responsible for taking animation from silent black-and-white cartoons with simple characters to full-color cartoons that featured synchronized sound and music and complex characters and clever effects. He steered animation away from the earlier "rubber hose" style of animated cartoons—where the characters' limbs seem to swing around like hoses attached to their bodies—to a more realistic and natural style of movement that is still used today.

Disney had a knack for developing characters that audiences loved: Donald Duck, Goofy, Pluto, and the most famous animated character of all time, Mickey Mouse. Early on, Mickey starred in one particular cartoon that represented a milestone in animation. Released in 1928, and drawn by the animator Ub Iwerks, *Steamboat Willie* was the first animated short to feature synchronized sound, a huge advance at the time. A live band played music while watching the cartoon, and the music was recorded to create a sound track that would match up with the animated action. The "multiplane" camera was devised by Disney's camera department to enhance the 3-D effect of their cartoons. Innovations like these allowed a quantum leap forward in animation technique, which wouldn't happen again until the advent of computer animation in the 1970s. In 1940, the Disney film *Fantasia* showed that animation could compete with painting and music and other forms of so-called high art. The film's beautiful images—not to mention its dancing hippos in tutus!—are set to music by classical composers such as Tchaikovsky, Beethoven, and Stravinsky.

Pencils, Ink, and Lots of Patience

Disney was a visionary pioneer, but his achievements were made possible by the army of creative and talented people he employed at his studio. Producing hand-drawn animation (and it was all hand-drawn, or 2-D, in the early days) is a laborious process. In addition to the animators, the team in an early animation studio included a director, writers, editors, storyboard artists, character designers, background artists, and camera operators. In the male-dominated world of the American animation studio, women were often assigned the lowly job of "inker," tracing over the draw-

FIND OUT MORE

In Pixar's animated film *Monsters, Inc.,* the restaurant is called "Harryhausen's" as a tribute to Ray Harryhausen. Learn more about this master animator at his Web site: http://www.rayharryhausen.com. Then rent the old movie *Jason and the Argonauts* (1963) and see Harryhausen's most famous stop-motion sequence: the incredible battle between Jason and the skeleton warriors.

ings in ink and painting the correct colors inside the outlines. Even those few women animators were paid less than men for the same work. All studio employees often worked long hours of overtime without pay, scrambling to meet production schedules as the demand for animated programs grew.

Imagination and a Steady Hand

As already mentioned, a traditional, or 2-D, animator works on thin sheets of paper with punched holes that fit over the pegs of a board with a pane of glass in the center. Under this glass is a light box. When the light shines through the paper, the animator can see the animation on four or five different sheets and gauge correctly the position of the next drawing. To cut down on work, only the parts of the character that move at a particular time will be redrawn: For instance, if the character is standing in one place and waving good-bye, only one hand and arm will need to be drawn; the unmoving body can just be traced over. Animators draw the extreme, or most important actions of the character; an "inbetweener" fills in the transitional motions between one extreme position and the next. These initial drawings serve as a kind of rough draft (called a *pencil test*) that will be photographed with an animation camera. The rough film will then be viewed by the animators, director, and story crew. Any necessary corrections can be made before the final animation art is created.

Once the pencil test has been approved, all the drawings are transferred (usually by photocopying) to transparent celluloid sheets, or "cels," and then painted on the reverse side. (Later, acetate replaced celluloid, which was dangerously flammable.) Backgrounds are also created for each scene, based on sketches made by the layout artists. When each cel is complete, it is photographed—one frame at a time—with a special animation camera, on

The Flying Horse

FIND OUT MORE

In the 1880s, a British photographer named Eadweard Muybridge settled the often debated question of whether all four legs of a racehorse leave the ground when the animal is galloping. Muybridge's sequence of photographs proved that they do indeed. His 1887 book, *Animal Locomotion*, is still a worthwhile resource for animators studying how humans and animals move. Have a look at these early images at http://en.wikipedia.org/wiki/Eadweard_Muybridge, then try drawing a movement sequence of five to six frames.

a peg board similar to what animators use. Camera operators follow the animator's instructions on an exposure sheet, which indicates how many exposures are needed per frame. Before the animation is completed, several sound tracks—some with music and some with dialogue—have been created. These tracks will be sent to a laboratory with the animated film footage, and a completed animated print combining images and sound will be created there.

Squash and Stretch—a Dynamic Duo

Animated films today still use the same basic principles developed at Disney Studios back in the 1930s. If you read about animation, a phrase you'll see often is "squash and stretch." The human body naturally squashes and stretches when performing different actions: When you sit down your body squashes, and when you stand up it stretches. Disney animators found that they could make an object look more lifelike by exaggerating these actions.

Another important animation technique is called "anticipation." Before a character moves in one direction, he anticipates that action by first pulling back in the opposite direction. Keep your eye out for this when you're watching an animated movie. A cartoon penguin jumping off an iceberg will first pull her little flippers back in the opposite direction before taking off. Anticipation makes all animated movement look more interesting and dramatic. Techniques like these were hallmarks of the Disney style that were imitated by other animation studios of the time.

Looney Tunes and Merrie Melodies

What people call the "Golden Age of Animation" peaked in the 1940s, when studios produced some of the best cartoons of all time. Next to Disney, Warner Bros. created scores of memorable characters, including Daffy Duck, Elmer Fudd, Porky Pig, and Bugs Bunny. Talents such as Isadore "Friz" Freleng, Tex Avery, and Chuck Jones had names nearly as colorful as the characters they brought to life. Warner Bros.' animated shorts, produced under the names of Looney Tunes and Merrie Melodies, were characterized by zany slapstick comedy that broke from the Disney style of more "naturalistic" animation. "Screwball" characters

FUN FACTOID

In 1997, Bugs Bunny was featured on a 32-cent postage stamp.

like Daffy Duck made audiences laugh with their wildly exaggerated actions and crazy antics. After all, why should animated characters have to obey the laws of physics? They can stretch and move in incredible ways, smoke a stick of dynamite, or squeeze through a tiny space and pop right back to their original shapes.

Creating Memorable Characters

Warner Bros. developed what many believe is the greatest cartoon character ever: that "wascally wabbit" Bugs Bunny. Voice actor Mel Blanc, "The Man of a Thousand Voices," gave Bugs a Brooklyn-meets-the-Bronx accent and a tough-guy attitude to match. Sometimes Blanc nibbled on carrots to get into character for the part. Bugs took 10 years to evolve into the character we recognize today with his signature tagline of "Eh, what's up, Doc?"

Another early form of direct animation features puppets or models that are filmed frame by frame and repositioned between frames, so the figures look like they are moving. This type of "stop-motion" animation was very popular in Eastern Europe, where there was a rich tradition of puppet theater. Czech animator Jiří Trnka, who died in 1969, is considered by many the best stop-motion animator in the world.

For the character of Jack Skellington, in Burton's *The Nightmare Before Christmas*, animators created 400 separate heads, each with a different expression. All 227 characters in the film had to be reposed after each take of the camera. The team working on this movie produced about 70 seconds of finished footage a week.

From Gumby to Gromit

Another variation of stop-motion animation, called *claymation*, uses plasticine modeling clay shaped around armatures, jointed metal skeletons that can be moved into countless positions. Working in front of the camera, animators shape each clay model into different positions from one frame to the next. Art Clokey's Gumby, that crazy green guy with the slanted head and the squeaky voice, introduced American audiences to claymation during the late 1950s. Animator Will Vinton is sometimes called "the Walt Disney of claymation" because he developed and re-

CHECK IT OUT

In Germany during the 1920s, an amazing artist named Lotte Reiniger (1899–1981) created animation using cut-paper silhouettes. She also used silhouettes to produce the first feature-length animated film, called *Prince Achmed*, in 1926.

fined this type of animation to a high art. Today Claymation is frequently featured in TV commercials, like the famous California Raisins, and is used to create the popular Wallace & Gromit films, from Academy Award-winning director Nick Park.

From the Big Screen to the Small

The art of animation made the transition to the new technology of television that began to invade American homes in the 1950s. In 1954, Walt Disney hosted *Disneyland* (later called *Disney's Wonderful World of Color*), a variety show featuring animated shorts from the studio's library. Cartoons such as Jay Ward's *Crusader Rabbit* were the first animated shorts made just for TV.

In the early 1950s, United Productions of American (or UPA) introduced the technique of "limited animation" in a film called *Gerald McBoing Boing*, which won the 1951 Academy Award for Best Animated Short. Limited animation was a reaction against Disney's naturalistic style. It used a reduced number of frames per second, recycled backgrounds, and restricted character motion (sometimes just the eyes and mouth moved). The 1968 film *Yellow Submarine*, based on the music of the Beatles and featuring psychedelic landscapes and bizarre characters, was created using limited animation.

Back then, TV animation houses were less interested in animation as an art form and more concerned with it as a money-maker. Producers like William Hanna and Joseph Barbera quickly glommed onto limited animation because it was much cheaper to produce than traditional animation. The quality of the animation on a Hanna-Barbera show like *Scooby-Doo* was generally poor, and the same story lines were used again and again, but viewers didn't seem to mind. By the mid-1960s, watching Saturday morning cartoons like *Huckleberry Hound* and *The Flintstones* had become a beloved weekly ritual for most American families.

Animation Nations

Around this time, animation began to take off in other countries, as well—especially in Canada, where the Nelvana studio was founded in 1971. Named after a Canadian comic book super-heroine from the 1940s, Nelvana produces children's animated programming that includes *The Fairly OddParents* and *Danny*

"I think CGI has the potential to equal or even surpass what the human hand can do."

—ANIMATOR HAYAO MIYAZAKI

Phantom. The Czech Republic has a rich tradition of animation. Celebrated Czech animators Jan Svankmajer and Zdenka Deitchova had to work under difficult conditions when the totalitarian government was strictly censoring artists' work. The communists even banned them from making films in the early 1970s. Perhaps because people thought animation was for kids and did not take it seriously, these artists were able to get around many rules and restrictions and create incredible work.

The country outside the United States that has influenced American animation the most is Japan. In the 1950s and 1960s, this nation saw an explosion in animation production and the development of very distinct and recognizable style featuring characters with huge eyes and dubbed voices. Americans got their first taste of the Japanese style of animation, called *anime*, when the cartoon show *Astro Boy* aired in 1963. Another popular show, *Speed Racer*, joined the Saturday morning lineup a few years later. The 1990s brought another surge of *anime* to the TV landscape, with the runaway success of the *Pokémon* show and trading cards as well as cartoons like *Sailor Moon* and *Yu-Gi-Oh*.

The Computer Revolution

Until the birth of the computer industry, and the development of software that allowed the user to draw and paint onscreen, the animation techniques developed by Disney and others early on did not change very much. Then, in 1961, an MIT student named Ivan Sutherland created an early computer drawing program called Sketchpad. About the same time, scientist Doug Englebart invented the computer mouse, which allowed people to interact with computers much more quickly and efficiently. It wasn't long before viewers were blown away by the thrilling, computer-generated special effects in live-action films like *Star Trek II, Last Starfighter,* and *Tron.*

But early computer animation was still rough-looking and not very impressive. At first, some traditional animators dismissed computer-generated imagery, or CGI, as a technological gimmick without a future.

Now computers have become a marvelous tool for animators, since they can be programmed to accomplish many of the most time-consuming tasks of the trade, such as doing the inbetweener's work, creating instant pencil tests, and filling in outlines with color.

Pixar-Perfect Animation

In 1996, a pair of computer-animated pals named Woody and Buzz Lightyear made an appearance at the 68th Annual Academy Awards. The year before they had starred in a "buddy picture" about a friendship between two toys that delighted audiences and demonstrated that computer animation had mastered the visual quality to compete with live-action films. Established in 1986 by Steve Jobs, founder of Apple Computer, the Pixar studio made animation history when it released *Toy Story,* the first fully computer-animated feature film and the highest grossing movie of 1995. Pixar teamed up with Disney to make a series of extremely successful computer-animated films including *Monsters, Inc., Finding Nemo,* and *The Incredibles.*

And Awaaaaay We Go!

As you read this book, computer animation is still in its early stages. New techniques are being developed every day. Who knows what marvels lie in store for us, at the click of a mouse! But traditional forms of animation, like 2-D and stop-motion, are still going strong, too. Shows like Trey Parker's *South Park* are intentionally rough and "low-tech," yet they attract masses of fans. What do you think the future of animation will look like? Probably just about anything you can imagine…and more.

CHECK IT OUT

The first animation on standard picture film was made by J. Stuart Blackton in 1906. Called *Humorous Phases of Funny Faces,* it features a cartoonist drawing different faces on a chalkboard, and the faces come to life. You can see this and other early films like *Gertie the Dinosaur* at the Library of Congress Web site: http://memory .loc/gov/ammem/ oahtml/oapres.html.

CHAPTER 2

Animator at Work

FUN FACTOID

Walt Disney's *Snow White and the Seven Dwarfs* (1937) is composed of approximately 477,000 individual drawings. If you added up all the hours that went into the artwork for this film, it would total about 200 years!

Animators have one of the most amazing jobs in the world. They use their imaginations to bring characters and stories to life. For the most part, whatever they can dream up, they can make "real" through animation. It's fun to make things happen that could never occur in real life—animators make superheroes fly across the sky, roadrunners race along the highway, and toy cowboys and spacemen thwart bad guys.

As an animator, it's incredibly fun to see your cartoons moving on TV, movie, or computer screens, but getting them there takes talent, teamwork, and long hours of hard work. *Finding Nemo* took five years and the efforts of hundreds of staff to produce.

An animator's job varies from day to day and depends on the position a person holds. But step behind the drawing board as a lead animator and you'll see that a typical day can be as action-packed and frantic as any cartoon.

Your Average, Crazy Day

The expression "back to the drawing board" really captures the work of an animator. As a lead animator, you must

"Don't ever lose PASSION! Don't EVER give up!"

—MARK ANDREWS, PIXAR FILMMAKER

constantly think about how your project is coming along, and you have to be willing to continually make changes and revisions to make your animation better. In a lecture at CalArts School of Film and Video, Ed Catmull, the president of Pixar animation studio, said that work on *Toy Story 2* took months of working day and night. Early on, after filming a reel, John Lasseter, the film's

Actors Tim Allen and Tom Hanks lent their voices to these *Toy Story* characters.

director, decided the story just wasn't working, so they scrapped the entire script and started from scratch. As a lead animator, you know that if you don't have a great story and appealing characters, it doesn't matter how well animated your project is. The whole thing can be a flop if you don't have a good story to tell.

As you work on a big feature film about a super-intelligent earthworm who becomes president of the United States, you begin your day in the conference room with the story writers, the producer, and the director, discussing the script and making sure that the story is working. You've already begun basic animation on the film, but you're still making changes to the script to make the best picture possible. You and the writers actually read some of the worm's lines aloud and act out some of its motions. This helps you gain a sense of how the animation will play out on screen.

A few weeks ago you were at the recording sessions when the voice actors recorded the script. The animators work from the recorded dialogue to make sure the actions of each animated character match what has been recorded. The voice director asked for your opinion on the actors' performances. He wanted to make sure the voice performances fit with your vision of how the characters should behave and sound on the big screen.

Even though a near-final script was recorded with actors, a few scenes seemed "flat." So during the morning meeting with the writers and director, you all agree on some new jokes and ways to improve the plot. The story writers head off to make revisions, and a few scenes with the voice actors will have to be recorded again.

A Talented Team

After this meeting you schedule another with your animators to review the scenes they've been working on. Your top animators have been creating storyboards, or rough drawings of the main points of action. They have filmed the storyboards and combined them with a recording of the actors reading the script and some preliminary music. This filmed version of the storyboards is called an *animatic*, or a *story reel*. The animatic is like a rough draft of the film that shows how the scenes are going to work together before the actual animation is done. You pay careful attention to all the details in the animatic, jotting down notes as you watch. You comment on the emotions being expressed by the charac-

FIND OUT MORE

The first Japanese animated film to grab an Oscar was animator Hayao Miyazaki's *Spirited Away*, which won the Academy Award for Best Animated Feature in 2002. Miyazaki's astonishing work, which includes *Princess Mononoke* and *Howl's Moving Castle*, should be required viewing for anyone really interested in this art form. You can read an interview with this master animator at http://www.midnighteye.com/interviews/hayao_miyazaki.shtml.

ters and how the characters' bodies and faces should be more dynamic. You look beyond the characters to the background settings and the objects in each scene. You tell your fellow animators what needs to be highlighted and what should be more realistic. You're thinking about the plot, the setting, and the angles for framing the action. You suggest where a camera should move in for a close-up on a character and where a camera should pull back from the main action. Your team will go back to the drawing board and make fixes to the storyboards before moving on to the final animation.

Animators create storyboards to sketch out ideas.

Other scenes from your movie are heading into final stages. Just like *The Simpsons* on TV, your animation is drawn by hand. You stop by a big, well-lit room filled with drawing tables where the assistant animators are hard at work. Some are working on walk cycles, others are cleaning up rough drawings created by you and other senior animators. These cleanup artists are adding in details and making stronger pencil lines on the key drawings before they're sent overseas to be fully animated. Cleanup artists keep a close eye on the drawings, watching for consistency in style and design, and note where different colors should go. Again, a team overseas will digitally paint and ink the animation following the instructions from your American team.

You also check in with your layout artists, who focus on making the backgrounds. Forests, cityscapes, the Oval Office—all the backdrops for the action are created by artists who specialize in backgrounds. The layout supervisor gives you a progress report, and you hustle back to your office for a call from your animation director in Korea.

The final stages of your animation project are typically done in Asia to save money. In Korea, your animation company hires a team of workers who complete the final touches. These animators take the key drawings that the American artists have made and then add in additional drawings called inbetweens, following instructions on a master sheet of directions known as an *exposure sheet*. The exposure sheet (also called the x-sheet) documents every action in an animated scene: It explains what is being filmed, gives camera directions, indicates what the voiceover should be saying and what music is playing. All departments working on the project refer to the exposure sheet and contribute their ideas by adding notes to it.

At the end of the day, you and the director and some of the lead animators gather together in a screening room to review a final edit of a few scenes. You watch with a very critical eye, and

Quick on the Draw

Get a sheet of paper and a pencil and draw a portrait of yourself while looking at your face in the mirror. Which of the following best describes the reactions you might get if your self-portrait were hanging on the wall of a museum?

A Get the guard—someone's scribbling graffiti on the wall!

B Oh, there's the sign for the ladies' room...or is it the emergency exit?

C Excuse me, can you tell me—oh, silly me! I mistook this picture for a real person!

D Ah, this is clearly the work of an outsider artist. Notice the crude lines, the clumsy shaping that seem to scream out, "Ugliness is the new beauty!"

Life drawing skills are crucial for animators. Even animators who work on computers need a solid understanding of how human and animal bodies are formed and how they move. If you have dreams of being an animator and you answered anything other than C, you'd better get back to the drawing board!

try to put yourself in the minds of your audience. You ask your-self: Is the action flowing smoothly? Are the voices and the char-acters working well together? Is the story holding your interest? Is there anything out of place on the screen? How is the music? You want the audience to feel swept up in the whole experience and not realize that they're watching an animated feature at all.

You're working long hours to deliver this movie in time for a summer release. Although animation is an artistic field, you have to be a bit of a businessperson as well. You keep an eye on budget, employee performance, and the schedule. As a respected supervisor on this film, you know that even as it nears comple-tion, your work will continue in areas that aren't related to the animation. The marketing staff will want your opinions on the content of the posters, the TV commercials, and the previews that will be shown in the theaters. Eventually, you may be asked to do interviews for TV, radio, newspapers, and magazines. In your spare time—when there is any—you read different animation magazines and check out Web sites, to keep up with the latest technologies and trends.

Even Big-Time Animators Start Small

The great thing about becoming an animator is that you can start simply. You just need two things: a pencil and paper. If your ideas are creative and people like them, you might become one of the most popular animators in the country. Matt Groening, the cre-ator of *The Simpsons*, began by stapling together little photo-copied books of his comics and handing them out for free. Now he's one of the most successful animators in history.

If you're serious about working in this field and want to get your hand in the door, you need a good education in art and ani-mation. As the old saying goes, practice makes perfect.

Animation Tech and Trends

Animation doesn't need sophisticated technology to exist. After all, you can draw a strolling stick figure on a pad of paper. But throughout animation history, technology has helped artists do their job more quickly and provided a way to reach a wider audience. Computers have made many aspects of animation easier. Workers can color in animation cels, generate in-between drawings, and build fantastic moving creatures within their hard drives. Some computer applications are so user-friendly that almost anyone can dive into the process and bring their imagination to life.

Check out some of the more cutting-edge technology and trends that have made an impact on the animation world. Keep in mind, though, that technology can't do the job for you. As John Lasseter, the director of *Toy Story* and *A Bug's Life*, said: "Technology doesn't make the motion picture, people do. You're not an animator just because you can move an object from point A to point B. You're someone who breathes life into a character which is something software and technology can't give you."

FUN FACTOID

The cartoon *Daria*, a spin-off from MTV's wildly popular animated series *Beavis and Butt-Head*, is unusual because the title character actually ages (from 16 to 18) during the series.

"Technology doesn't make the motion picture, people do."

—JOHN LASSETER, DIRECTOR

Capturing Motion with a Computer

A revolutionary technique that has made animation more realistic than ever is called motion capture, or mocap. Mocap lets filmmakers digitize all the movements of a real performer. The performer wears special pads that identify positions of the body,

Using a blend of high-tech computer and low-tech pen to make preliminary sketches for an animated cartoon.

track motion, and record facial expressions. Then it zaps that information into the computer. With all these details recorded about the performer's motions, the animator can then build a character over the now-digitized performer. Filmmakers recorded the routines of tapdancer Savion Glover with mocap for the movie *Happy Feet*. Through computer technology, Glover transformed into Mumble the penguin, who can't sing but can move with great agility. Another wonderful example of mocap is *The Polar Express*, starring the motion-captured Tom Hanks.

Computer Animation Meets Live Action

Computer-generated imagery is not just for producing animated films like *Shrek*. CGI has brought to life beasts, aliens, monsters, and more in many live-action movies. *Terminator*, *Independence Day*, *Star Wars*, and *The Matrix* are all major motion pictures that depend on CGI. *Jurassic Park* is one of the best examples. The realistic dinosaurs in this movie are a combination of CGI-animated creatures and large mechanical models known as *animatronics*. Basically, an animatronic is a mechanized puppet. *Jurassic Park* was made by blending images of the animatronic dinosaurs with digital versions created by computer animation experts. If you ever see *Jurassic Park*, the close-ups of the dinosaurs are usually animatronics and any scenes that show the entire creature moving across the screen is usually CGI animation.

Koko the Rotoscoped Clown

Today, computers are used to capture the realistic motions of performers, but animators developed another type of motion capture back in 1914. When Max Fleischer animated Koko the Clown for his Out of the Inkwell series, he filmed his brother Dave dressed in a clown outfit and then traced his motions frame by frame using special projection equipment called a *rotoscope*. Rotoscoping has been used effectively to animate the human characters in many Disney films—Snow White and Cinderella both started out as real actresses who were rotoscoped. In 1994, a digital rotoscoping technique was invented that lets a computer change the frames of live action into a drawn or animated look. Although not used much, this technique can be found in some video games and movies.

Working with live animals to create movies like *Babe: Pig in the City* comes with its own special challenges.

Acting with Cartoons

Very early on in the history of animation, filmmakers figured out a way that cartoons and live actors could interact on screen. In an early movie version of *Alice in Wonderland*, a live actress interacts with all animated characters. In *Anchors Aweigh*, Gene Kelly dances with Jerry the Mouse from *Tom and Jerry*, and in *Mary Poppins*, the actors dance and sing with cartoon penguins and other characters. To achieve this effect, animators overlaid animated cels on the live-action frames. *Who Framed Roger Rabbit* took the idea to a new level, using advanced "visual compositing techniques" to blend the actions between cartoons and people in a more realistic way. At its release, it was one of the most expensive films ever made.

Talk to the Animals

If you've seen the live-action movies *Babe*, *Charlotte's Web*, or *Racing Stripes*, you may wonder how those critters can seem to talk—moving their mouths in the exact patterns of the words you hear. Computer animation is again the answer. Animators take a computer-generated image of each animal's head and manipulate their faces using Maya and other software. Software is so advanced now that there is even a specific application for creating realistic computerized fur called *Furocious*.

The Game Explosion

Computer, video, and Internet games have become huge business. Sales have eclipsed the film industry, bringing in more than $10 billion a year. Because these games rely on the most sophisticated computer animation to make them as cinematic as possible, today's video game creators not only need all the same skills as TV and film animators, they also have to understand game play and what goes into making a fun game. With improved art, story lines, and special effects, games are becoming a serious art form, and even big directors like Steven Spielberg and Peter Jackson are "directing" games.

The YouTube Revolution

If you're a beginner animator, times have never been better to have your work seen by a wide audience. You can easily post animations constructed in the simple Flash program on the Web, and you can especially reach masses through YouTube .com. A homemade video of two boys lip-synching the *Pokémon* theme song was watched more than 9.5 million times in four months on YouTube. So if you've got a good idea for a cartoon, get going. You could be a YouTube hit.

Life Savers

One of the exciting new applications for animation is in the field of medicine. Computer animations of the human body can show medical students how to perform

Whatchamacallit-scope?

Early experiments in animation resulted in a dizzying array of devices such as the mutoscope. Construct one of the simplest of these—the thaumatrope, invented in 1825—and see for yourself how it works. You'll need a small cardboard disk (about 2 inches in diameter) and two short pieces of string. Use a pin to poke two small holes at the edges of the disk, directly across from each other. Thread a string through each hole and knot it securely to hold the strings in place on either side of the disk. Draw a small fish on one side and a round, empty fishbowl on the other. Then twist the strings tight and stretch them between your fingers to make the disk spin back and forth. What happens to the fish?

FIND OUT MORE

different surgical procedures and help doctors explain medical procedures to their patients. Computer animation helped a young Canadian boy stricken with cerebral palsy to walk again. Animations of his skeleton and muscles gave doctors an accurate picture of the corrective surgeries they needed to perform.

DIY Animation

If you want to be an animator, just do it! Do-it-yourself animation software is easily available and increasingly affordable or even free on the Web. You can learn both traditional and computer animation skills onscreen. When you've mastered some techniques you can create and distribute your own animated shorts via the Internet. Software such as Flash Animation and Web sites such as Larry's Toon Institute on the Animation Worldwide Network (http://tooninstitute.awn.com), let you download free animation lessons at the click of a mouse.

Indies and Outies

People have always been attracted to animation as an art form because it can go beyond the limits of the live-action film. (As rubbery as he is, Jim Carrey can't twist himself into a pretzel without the help of some pretty special effects.) The availability of animation software has fueled a wave of independent animators who can take risks and try things that the big studios can't or won't do. Animation festivals are a great place to see what indie animators are dreaming up.

In a Flash

Flash animation is an animated film distributed via the Internet in the .swf file format of Adobe Flash animation software The program uses limited animation, so movements aren't very fluid or natural. But even though motions are limited, the animation can still be fun and lively. *Ren & Stimpy* creator John Kricfalusi used Flash animation to bring cartoons (sometimes called *online cartoons* or *webtoons*) to the Internet. The hilarious Flash animated 'toons created by brothers Mark and Mike Chapman on their Web site http://www.homestarrunner.com attracted a big online audience. Some lucky fans even got to see their own e-mails turned into cartoons starring the show's masked villain, Strong Bad.

FIND OUT MORE

If you catch any old episodes of *The Tracey Ullman Show*, you'll see that the original *Simpsons* were a pretty rough bunch! (Go to http://en.wikipedia.org/wiki/Image: Simpsons_on_ Tracey_Ullman.png to see a picture of cartoonist Matt Groening's earliest version of *The Simpsons*.) Can you think of other cartoon characters that have been "cutified" over time?

POP QUIZ

Learn Anything Yet?

You've already read about the answers to the following questions. How many can you get right?

1 A phenomenon called "persistence of _____" makes the art of animation possible.

2 The first full-length computer-animated feature film was called _____ and featured two memorable characters named Woody and Buzz.

3 Mickey Mouse, the most famous animated character in history, debuted with sound in a 1928 Disney short cartoon called _____.

4 To bring their characters to life, animators often use a technique called "squash and _____."

5 The term "mocap" is short for a technique in computer animation called _____ that uses sensors placed on live actors' bodies to transfer realistic motion into cyberspace.

ANSWERS: 1-vision, 2-Toy Story, 3-Steamboat Willie, 4-stretch, 5-motion capture

Even some of today's popular TV animations are constructed with Flash, including *Foster's Home for Imaginary Friends*.

The Animator Did It

Another interesting use of computer animation is in the field of forensic science, which is the study of evidence found at crime scenes. Working from a skeleton or skull, forensics experts can now use animation software to re-create the faces of crime victims. Animated sequences can also be created to help a jury visualize how a crime might have occurred.

Annie Get Your Award

Once considered sort of a visual appetizer before the live-action feature, today animation is regarded as a legitimate art form that

ANIMATION TECH AND TRENDS

pulls in huge receipts at the box office and enjoys its very own annual awards ceremony. The Annie Awards, sponsored by ASI-FA-Hollywood, represent "animation's highest honor." Recent Annies for Best Animated Features went to *Wallace & Gromit: The Curse of the Were-Rabbit*, *Madagascar*, and *Howl's Moving Castle*.

Bugs Bunny, Spokesrabbit

In Southeast Asia, children are injured or killed every year by land mines buried back during the Vietnam War. A Cambodian film warning about the dangers of land mines featured Bugs Bunny as its spokesperson. The "rascally rabbit" was chosen not because he's so clever at escaping from the not-so-dangerous Elmer Fudd but because, in Cambodia, rabbits are considered intelligent and kind.

Outsourcing Animation

American corporations often hire workers in other countries where wages are lower than in the United States. Recently, more animation studios have followed this lead: To cut production costs, a lot of character animation is not done in the United States anymore, but is "outsourced" to animators in countries such as China, Korea, the Philippines, and India.

CHAPTER 4

Serious Training for a Funny Business

When you're busy laughing at Scooby-Doo or jumping up and down on the couch watching *Monster House*, you don't notice all the hard work that goes into the action on screen. Slow down a really good cartoon and pause on a single scene. Look at the background, the colors, the shape of the character and the lines used to create it. You can see that each frame is a work of art. The character may be goofy but the artistic technique needed to create it is very serious.

In some ways, artists are born. Many love drawing from an early age and churn out piles of cartoons and doodles even as children. Animation requires thousands of drawings, so you want to be able to easily produce a mountain of drawings, and you should love doing it. Basically, if you don't love to draw, you might not want to plunge headfirst into an animation career. (Still, there are related jobs in the field for non-artists—check out the next chapter for some great ideas.)

In middle school and high school, you can work toward becoming an animator by taking art classes and starting to learn the fundamentals of art. Draw your own comics. Try making your own flipbooks. Also, watch your favorite cartoons with a

CHECK IT OUT

One of the best ways to learn about the craft is to watch other animators do their stuff. Rent a classic animated film like Disney's *Pinocchio* on DVD and watch selected scenes one frame at a time to learn a lot about this art form.

critical eye. Ask yourself why you enjoy these shows. Many software programs are readily available that make animating on the computer easy. Although drawing and animating on your own can get you started, a higher education provides the serious training you need to sharpen your skills.

Many aspiring cartoon animators hone their creative talents in high school art classes.

CHECK IT OUT

The Disney Way

The 12 principles of character animation, as developed at the Disney studio:

1. Squash and stretch. (Shape distortion to accentuate movement)
2. Anticipation. (Reverse movement to accent a forward movement)
3. Staging. (The camera viewpoint to best show the action)
4. Straight-ahead vs. pose-to-pose action. (Two basic procedures)
5. Follow-through and overlapping action. (Nothing stops abruptly)
6. Slow-in and slow-out. (Smoothing starts and stops by spacing)
7. Arcs. (Planning the path of actions)
8. Secondary actions. (A head might wag while the legs walk)
9. Timing. (Time relations within actions for the illusion of life)
10. Exaggeration. (Caricature of actions and timing)
11. Solid drawing. (Learn good drawing to be a good animator)
12. Appeal. (If the characters are not appealing, then all is lost)

Fine Art Fundamentals

With a few exceptions, most animators have first learned traditional art and drawing techniques before producing an animated work. Even though computer technology can make the animation process easier, animators rely on solid drawing and art skills to create animals, humans, backgrounds, and objects. Although college isn't necessary, animators often hone their artistic talents in a two- or four-year program. In college, they focus on drawing from real life—concentrating on proportions, measurements, and angles. They learn how to use shadows, shading, and perspective to make things appear three-dimensional even on a two-dimensional plane. With practice artists learn to twist what they see in real life to conjure up their own exaggerated characters.

College classes include 2-D design fundamentals, the history of media arts, life drawing, analysis of form, color fundamentals, layout, design and concept, story development, acting for animators, and animal drawing. Budding artists learn techniques in the classroom but, just like musicians, they perfect them with practice, practice, and more practice.

Beyond the hands-on art training, students take courses in art history to observe the techniques of the masters and get ideas for their own creations. Top animators who create hit series or movies also are great storytellers. Courses in writing and literature can help you become good at weaving your own tales. John Andrews, creative director at the commercial animation studio ka-chew!, reviews the work of many student animators. He says that strong storytelling is a skill that many of today's students desperately need to develop. You can develop story-writing skills now by writing your own tales and paying attention to the writing on films and television series. Take note of which ones you especially enjoy and why the stories are so good.

Because cartoons are the actors in these films, animators often study acting techniques and movement so they can have their characters give convincing performances. In fact, Pixar's Web site says, "A Pixar animator should be able to bring life to any object or character, showing the character's internal thoughts and feelings through its physical external motion. To do this, the animator must be a good actor." Who knows? Maybe one day in the future, an animated character will accept the Oscar for best actor or actress!

A basic understanding of physics helps animators, too. They need to know the principles of motion: If a character gets socked in the jaw, how might he fly through the air? What arc would he follow? Principles of light are equally important: If the sun is setting, where is the character's shadow and how long should it be? The science of sound also figures into the picture: If a heavy anvil falls to the ground, how loud is the thud? When Wile E. Coyote falls down a tall cliff, the crash sound is noticeably off in the distance. Finally, some education of human and animal anatomy can help as well, to better understand how humans and other creatures really look and move. This tantalizing mix of real and imaginary is what makes cartoons so fun!

Animation A-Z

Students, of course, also learn animation fundamentals. How do you produce a series of drawings that will show motion? Actions in animation are often exaggerated, and artists must learn standard approaches. Storyboards, key frames, in-betweens, clean-up, musical scoring—all the elements that an animator combines into a final product—are taught in college programs.

Basic animation training can begin with sequence drawing. Here, students figure out how a character's entire body moves when it goes through different actions. Because the most common action is walking, you usually create something called a *walk cycle* for each character. You draw each key frame of the motion, and then the walk sequence is used as a reference every time the

Aspiring animators find inspiration in unusual places such as human anatomy classes.

character walks, As an animator-in-training, you will also develop a skill for capturing facial expressions, which are vital for conveying emotions. That's why life drawing classes are so helpful. If you practice putting various moods on paper, you can apply that talent to future creations. Plus, drawing from life can be a great source of inspiration for your imaginary creatures.

Another basic art principle in animation is called *composition*. You want scenes to look balanced, and your character should be the focus. You also have to think of the frames you draw in a cinematic manner. Think of the angles at which you're framing your art. Will your viewer see things from above, below, or straight on? Also, do you want your action to zoom in or out, or pan left or right? Your characters will need a setting or environment to interact in as well, so you need to learn how to generate backgrounds, which might be in outer space, underwater, or on a farm. Backgrounds can't distract from your main action, so artists learn to create them in a "gestural" form, which conveys the setting without getting too detailed.

Characters, too, should not be overly detailed or they will be impossible to draw over and over again. For each character, you develop a model sheet showing its basic features—body design, facial expressions, and three to five neutral views of the character showing him or her from different angles. Characters today are sometimes sculpted in clay to create a model or *maquette*. Animators use 3-D maquettes as a reference for all character drawings. Maquettes can be scanned for computer animation as well.

With a firm grasp of art fundamentals—especially a strong line and a good design sense, animators can take the first steps toward developing their own animations. First you'll need a story. With a simple story in mind, you make storyboards showing the main scenes of action in your animation.

Creature Feature

Good animators are close observers of reality. To beef up your own drawing skills, create a reference file: Cut out pictures of all kinds of animals and collect them in a folder. Practice sketching different creatures while studying these images, to better understand how each animal's body fits together and moves. Also, watch nature shows on TV. Pay careful attention to how various animals behave and how they react. Do they hold their tails up or down when they run? Do they crouch when they eat? A grasp of these details can really bring your animated critters to life.

As you progress along, churning out your drawings, you stop now and then to flip through and make sure your animation has the action and look that you want. Some animators use a "pencil-test system" to review their sequences. This allows them to see their preliminary animation on the screen. Once your rough animation is entirely correct, you move on to cleanup drawing. Cleanup takes the rough animation and makes it perfect.

Once you have a series of drawings that will look great animated, how do you get them on film? Animators must know how cameras are used to film their work. They also learn how audio is combined with their work—bringing in the voices of the characters, the sound effects, and music. An animator's training is similar to a filmmaker's because that's exactly what you're trying to do—make an effective film. You have to understand what looks good on the screen and how images will drive your story forward.

When you graduate, you should leave school with a good demo reel—a sample of what you can do in animation. You'll also want a portfolio showing your strengths and diversity, containing figure drawing, character sketches, and painting.

Computer Smarts

Computer animation has really exploded over the past 20 years—especially for feature-length movies and on some television series, such as *Jimmy Neutron*. Even traditional hand-drawn animations get the computer touch nowadays—animators use computers to "paint" in color, ink drawing, and even fill out some sequences. In many ways, computers have sped up the process of animation, but they have also introduced a whole new set of skills that animators must master.

Computer animation is often referred to as CGI (for computer-generated imagery), and it follows the basic principles of all animation. You make one frame of art and then slightly change it in the next frame, until you have a series of frames that create an illusion of motion. The computer can aid an animator's job, but you can't rely on technology to do the work for you. In 3-D animation, you learn how to create "models" of characters and objects in the computer. You "rig" the characters with a virtual skeleton and then add layers of muscle, clothes, color, light, and

REALITY CHECK

If you've ever made a flipbook, you know that even the simplest effect can take many drawings to produce. Animation is incredibly time consuming. (Remember: There are 24 frames in just one second of film.) If you're an impatient person who demands quick results, this job might drive you nuts.

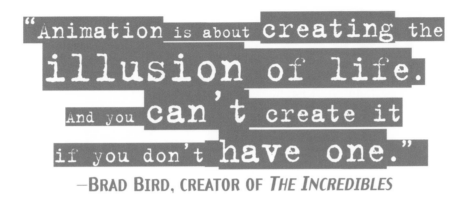

"Animation is about creating the illusion of life. And you can't create it if you don't have one."

—Brad Bird, creator of *The Incredibles*

shadowing. The position of a character's every feature is defined by an *avar* (short for *animation variable*). To create Woody in *Toy Story*, animators used 700 avars–100 of these were used in Woody's face alone to give him such great facial expressions. The computer allows the animator to manipulate the avars to create the character movements.

Special programs let the user apply textures, shading, lighting, and other effects. The differences in appearance between key frames are automatically calculated by the computer in a process known as *tweening*, or *morphing*. Finally, the animation is rendered, which means the images are given their final detailed appearance.

Two-dimensional animation can be done on a computer as well. The moving objects are often referred to as sprites. A common 2-D animation program called Macromedia Flash is often used for simple Internet-based animations.

Versatile computer animators can also find work outside of animated movies. Many of today's action films use computer animators to generate their special effects. Movies such as *Charlie and the Chocolate Factory* and *Night at the Museum* all depend on the latest CGI techniques. Do you like video games? The computer games industry needs computer animators, too.

CHAPTER 5

Filling in the Background

Animators may dream up hit characters

like Nemo and Taz, but it takes a team of many specialized workers to bring these characters to life. As you will see from these related careers, many different jobs are in this industry for people who love animation—even for those who can't draw at all. Check out the list below and see if any of these occupations match your talents and interests.

Animation Checker

Checkers are like the proofreaders of animation. Checkers look over the final instructions sent to the studios that actually film the final animation. Animation studios receive a scene folder that holds all the key drawings that show the main actions of the characters. The folder also includes timing sheets that explain what's happening in every moment of the film. The checker looks over these materials to make certain nothing is missing. She may notice that a character is saying, "Youccch!!!" but the mouth motion is not listed in the instructions. It's the checker's job to catch these mistakes and make sure they're fixed before the animation goes into final production.

> **"Computer animators just have a fancy electric pencil—you still have to know how to draw."**
>
> —FRANK GLADSTONE, DISNEY ANIMATION TRAINING MANAGER

Animation Director

The overall look and direction of a project is in the hands of the animation director. Animation directors are almost always former animators who are now in charge of other animators. They make sure that the animators working on a project are sticking to the specific style required and creating the necessary drawings. They make sure the final edit matches the final script. Directors often have a say in script changes, acting, audio effects, music, and all the elements that go into a production.

Animation Teacher

This original pen-and-paper business has evolved over the years, so today's animators have many new tools to learn. They need to master computer programs to create 3-D cartoons, shadings, and backgrounds. Teachers train budding animators to use the latest software, but they also teach students the fundamentals of art and design. To be a great animator you still need to know how to do figure drawing, cartooning, painting, shading, and other art basics. Teachers are experienced animators and artists who enjoy showing others how to develop their unique talents.

Animation Timer

This professional determines how many frames it's going to take for a character to make each action. If a character is raising her right hand from her waist to her head, the animation timer calculates that that action may be done in eight frames or a quarter of a second. (The standard rule is that 24 frames of film are

NAME: John Derevlany

OFFICIAL TITLE: Story Editor

What Do You Do?

I'm a story editor, which, in animation, really means head writer. I'm working on the TV animated show *Gerald McBoing Boing* and an animated version of Louis Sacher's *Wayside School* and something called *Monster Buster Club*. I write, I assign other writers, and I rewrite their work. I may have writing coming in from as many as 20 different writers, and I have to make sure their writing is consistent and right for each show. For an animated series, we'll film 52 11-minute scripts. There can be a total of six drafts for an episode of any show. The script will go to network executives, and they may ask for certain changes in their show, so they'll send back notes.

It's a very creative job. You come up with story lines. Sometimes you come up with characters. I'll go to voice-over sessions because I want to write to the actors' strengths and weaknesses. I give suggestions for music and I cowrote the theme songs for a couple shows. There's a certain amount of selling in this job, too—pitching your ideas.

How Did You Get Started?

I used to make little stop-motion movies with G.I. Joes and with clay figures as a kid. Then I got into writing different things for TV and I worked with Michael Moore on a show called *TV Nation*. On that show, I was Crackers, the Corporate Crime-Fighting Chicken. I wore a big chicken suit. Because of that, the Henson people and a cartoon called *The Angry Beavers* hired me. The most important thing about animation is your ability to tell a story. It's not just gags.

If you want to get into this business, watch as many shows as you can and try to outline the story. Figure out how it works. If I were in middle school today, I'd be making my own little films and putting them on YouTube.

ON THE JOB

What's My Line?

Which famous catchphrase is each of these animated characters known for?

1 ▶ Fred Flintstone
2 ▶ Betty Boop
3 ▶ Kyle or Stan
4 ▶ Popeye
5 ▶ Fat Albert
6 ▶ Homer Simpson
7 ▶ Sylvester the Cat
8 ▶ Bugs Bunny

A ▶ "I yam what I yam."
B ▶ "Oh my god, they killed Kenny!"
C ▶ "Hey hey hey!"
D ▶ "Yabba dabba doo!"
E ▶ "Thufferin' thuccotash!"
F ▶ "D'oh."
G ▶ "Eh, what's up, Doc?"
H ▶ "Boop-oop-a-doop!"

ANSWERS: 1-D, 2-H, 3-B, 4-A, 5-C, 6-F, 7-E, 8-G

needed to create one second of an animated film.) Every single motion, even the smallest detail, has to be recorded so everyone knows where the action is and how many frames it will take to animate it. Animation timers write out information on character animation, dialogue, and camera movements on an exposure sheet. Each department records their contribution to the scene on this sheet.

Assistant Animator

Most senior animators start with an entry-level position helping more experienced animators. Assistants often learn the basics by drawing backgrounds, cleaning up the finals, helping on storyboards, or drawing the inbetweens. As an assistant, you have a chance to see the entire production process and learn the techniques and lingo of the trade. After getting up to speed as an assistant, you can start to plan your own animated scenes. A lot of today's top animators started out as assistants, including Butch Hartman, who went on to create *The Fairly OddParents* and *Danny Phantom*.

Music Composer

The mood in an animated feature can easily be set by the music playing in the background—a pulsating rock song can intensify a fight scene or strings playing slowly can make a sad moment even sadder. Composers watch scenes in cartoons and come up with the appropriate music to match. They often work closely with a sound designer to make sure their musical score meshes with the sound effects that the designer is putting in.

Producer

Producers in animation are like producers of live-action features. They head the entire production process and make sure the animation gets made on time and on budget. They may work closely with the director to accomplish this. The producer is often in charge of putting together a crack team to complete the job and sometimes has a hand in raising money for a project, too. A producer often wears many different hats, overseeing all different activities that go into the final production. A background in business management and the arts can help, and several colleges now offer degrees in arts management.

Production Assistant

If you're young, love cartoons, but aren't necessarily artistic, you can do some close-up career exploration as a production assistant. While assistants do many of the menial tasks required, such as photocopying, they may also lend a hand to all the different departments. Assistants can get hands-on experience and make personal connections needed to advance in the field.

Publicist/Marketer

TV shows, movies, and video games all need a public to view them. Professionals in this field work to make sure animation is seen by as many people as possible. Publicists are great communicators—many write press releases and talk to entertainment writers about the latest shows they're working on. Some marketers work on marketing programs such as product tie-ins. Have you seen Jimmy Neutron's weird head on a can of soup or your favorite cartoon characters on a box of cereal? These product

CHECK IT OUT

Author Dav Pilkey uses some of the basic principles of animation in his goofy Captain Underpants series. Pilkey's patented "Flip-O-Rama" technique, where the reader is instructed to flip back and forth between two different cartoon images, creating the illusion of movement, relies on the phenomenon of persistence of vision to work.

NAME: Robin Cooper

OFFICIAL TITLE: Digital Painter/Shader/Art Director

What Do You Do?

I've worked at Pixar for 11 years as a digital painter, shader, and art director. The director John Lasseter loves detailed digital painting and I painted on *Toy Story*, *Toy Story 2*, and *A Bug's Life*. I did preproduction art on *Monsters, Inc.* and art direction on *Finding Nemo*. As a digital shader, I add "interest" to the surface of objects and characters. Anything that goes on the surface of an object in a 3-D film is called shading. You have to be technical and artistic to do good shading.

One of the best parts of my job as an art director has been initial research, especially on *Nemo*. I studied how scales on fish work and the optics of color underwater. We talked about which colors last the longest as fish go off in a distance and how they look in the murk. You take in all this information and see how it's relevant to your process. Everything you do in shading and art direction is subordinate to the animation and the story. Animation is an intense field and hours are long—more than 60- or 70-hours some weeks. There's an intensity in each project. You're trying to reach a deadline and quality. There are a lot of people involved. We made *Toy Story* with about 150 people and now there are anywhere from 800 to 900 people involved in each Pixar movie.

It's so fun when the movie is in the theaters. Especially *Toy Story*—we didn't know how big it was going to be. People around the world know who Nemo is. It's been a surprise to make a good living as an artist.

How Did You Get Started?

I started acting in high school and in college I wanted to get a degree in directing in theater. But I discovered that I could paint at San Francisco State College. I loved it. I got a degree in set design, but it's hard to make a living at that. I painted all over the Bay Area—in community theater, the opera,

store window displays, and home interiors. Then a friend of mine at Pixar asked if I would come in and give a talk on traditional scenic painting. They liked my presentation so when they decided they needed a second digital painter, they asked me to interview. I didn't know the computer but I produced a lot of hand-painted samples—wood samples, granite samples, concrete. They were impressed with my art skills, hired me, and taught me how to paint and shade using the computer.

NAME: John Andrews

OFFICIAL TITLE: Creative Director/Producer

What Do You Do?

I assemble the team in the animation process. I use my judgment to creatively cast a project—choosing the right technical people, designers, background artists, animators, coordinators, voice talent, and composers. I also get the business and make presentations to a potential client.

A couple of years ago we began doing TV commercials for a product called Mucinex that has a character called Mr. Mucus. Initially, we were asked to submit designs for what Mr. Mucus would look like, along with a budget and schedule. Other companies made submissions, but the client liked our ideas best so we got the job.

A lot of the animation process is identical to shooting a live-action film but shrunk down to within the computer box. Mr. Mucus is a computer character, but he was thoroughly designed on paper with pencil. So, even though our work starts with a simple process, it goes high-tech pretty quick.

ON THE JOB

How Did You Get Started?

I had come from a background in theater. I got started in animation working for an audiovisual company. We'd make animation by moving quickly from one slide to another. Then I did simple digital animations on a TV show called *Adam Smith's Money World*. I learned on the job, and I became the "go-to" guy for graphics and animation. Gradually, I got to know a lot of animators, designers, and illustrators. When MTV wanted a producer to produce the *Beavis and Butt-Head* series, a friend of mine at Nickelodeon called me and I was hired. I did a lot of quick learning about how an animated series is produced. I put together a team that could move a lot of production through a studio at a rapid pace, and I learned how to work with overseas partners to do parts of the animation. I went on to do *Daria* and I co-produced the Beavis and Butt-Head film. That was a challenge to take something that was simple animation for the small screen and make it into something that could play on the big screen.

tie-ins help promote those animations. Toy companies, fast-food chains, and other businesses often want to use popular cartoons to sell their products, and they'll pay big dollars to do so. As a marketer, you might handle these types of business deals.

Sound Designer

The fun of animation is not just the visuals. Close your eyes sometime and just listen to the wild sounds that go into a production. When someone throws a tomato, explodes some dynamite, or is surprised enough to have his eyes pop out of his head, it just wouldn't be the same without the squish, boom, or boing. The exaggerated motions we see on screen are often matched with exaggerated sounds. A cartoon like *The Road Runner Show* depends entirely on sound effects because it has no dialogue. Often, sound editors use prerecorded sound effects or they have built their own library of sounds. Sometimes, though, the action on screen needs a distinct sound, and the sound designer will have to record it on the spot. A specialist called a Foley artist (named for Jack Foley, a sound effects pioneer) creates natural "everyday" sounds for the sound designer. To enter this career it helps to have an education in audio engineering. Some schools even offer degrees in sound design.

Splat! Bang! Boom!

Sound effects add energy and mood to any cartoon. Here's how some of the classic sounds of animation are created by sound designers and Foley artists:

- Batting eyes—a trill on the piano
- Horse gallop—coconut shells banged together
- Crackling fire—crumpling up cellophane
- Bird wing flaps—flapping a pair of gloves
- Snow crunch—stepping on corn starch in a leather pouch

Voice Talent

Imagine SpongeBob without his high crazy voice, or Fred Flintstone without his distinctive "Yabba-dabba-doo!!" Actors definitely give an animated character its distinctive personality. Some actors in the animation world specialize in creating different character voices. The actor Dan Castellaneta is the voice of Homer Simpson, Grandpa, Groundskeeper Willie, and Krusty the Clown, to name a few. Sometimes a male character will even be voiced by a woman—especially if the character is a boy. Jimmy Neutron is voiced by Debi Derryberry. Actors often get parts in cartoons by auditioning—just like they would for a movie, play, or TV show. Sometimes, those who specialize in voice acting make a "demo" of all the different styles of voices they can do. More and more animated characters are being voiced by known celebrities (Tom Hanks was Woody in *Toy Story*, Ben Stiller was the Lion in *Madagascar*). If you want to explore the career further, check out the American Voice Talent Association at http://www.americanvoicetalentassociation.com.

Writer

At the core of any successful animated film or TV show is a good story—that's what makes you care about the characters and want to know what will happen next. Writing a script for animation is different from writing for live action: Typically, there is much more action to describe, and jokes are often delivered rapid fire. Brad Bird, who created *The Incredibles*, says, "You want to be a storyteller that makes people forget that they're watching a movie." If you're interested in becoming an animation writer, the most important thing is to keep writing. Make up stories, keep a journal, enter contests. Eventually, you'll have to learn standard script formats, and there are many guides out there to help. Look at animated scripts, too. You can find many online. The entire script for *The Lion King* is available for free at http://www.lionking.org/scripts. Or, you can purchase screenwriting software to help you do the job. Those who are super-serious about the career may pursue a college degree in screenwriting.

It's hammerspace time! In Japanese cartoons, a female character will often produce a wooden rice mallet out of thin air and clonk it on the head of any man who has angered or insulted her. This familiar scene from anime is the origin of the term *hammerspace*, used in the world of animation. Hammerspace is a sort of extra dimension that characters pull objects out of: a mallet, a catapult, or a bomb labeled "ACME."

NAME: Rich Horvitz
OFFICIAL TITLE: Voiceover Artist

What Do You Do?

On Cartoon Network, I am the voice of Billy on *The Grim Adventures of Billy and Mandy,* Grey Matter on *Ben 10*, and Squirrel Boy on a new series called *Squirrel Boy*. A typical voice recording session is fun and hilarious.

A couple days before recording, you receive the script and read it over. You may meet with the other voice actors to do a "table read" first and make notes about how you're going to perform it. Then we go into the studio and read the scripts. I have to take good care of my voice. I drink a lot of tea and water.

How Did You Get Started?

I started acting professionally at age 10. I started out doing *Oliver* in theater. Then I did commercials and guest spots on shows like *Diff'rent Strokes* and *Head of the Class*. I was always told I have an interesting voice. But after I had fairly good success as a kid and young adult, I kept losing out on parts because casting people kept saying, "His voice doesn't match his looks."

That led me into animation voice-over acting. I made a demo reel and got an agent. I immediately booked three commercials. I had one word in each one. But then I didn't work the rest of the year. I finally got a regular part on *The Angry Beavers*. I did 62 episodes of that and that was really my big break. Voiceover work is really about the acting. You can have a funny voice but you have to have the acting chops behind it.

ON THE JOB

I have to take **good care** of my **voice**...I drink a lot of tea and water.

CHAPTER 6

Kids Ask, Animators Answer

It's no surprise that kids love animation.

To get the real deal on being an animator, we asked students in Holly VanEis's eighth-grade language arts class at J. Frank Dobie Middle School in Austin, Texas. We posed their questions to two working animators. Yvette Kaplan is an animator and director who worked on the TV series *Doug*, *The Magic School Bus*, and *Cyberchase*, and the movies *Ice Age* and *Happily Never After*. Tom Sorem is an independent computer animator who has worked on many different commercials, including M&Ms and the California Raisins, as well as on the movie *The Polar Express* starring Tom Hanks.

Why did you start doing animation?

–Chelsea A., age 13

Yvette: I was five years old when I decided to get into animation. I drew constantly. I made up characters. I made up stories–comic strips and little books. I grew up in Bensonhurst, Brooklyn, and I was lucky there were art teachers. But I was a big cartoon fan. I must have seen a *Wonderful World of Disney* episode that showed the process of animation and I decided then that being an animator was for me.

Tom: I grew up in Pullman in eastern Washington, and art was always at the forefront of my interests. I got into ani-

> # "I drew constantly. I made up characters. I made up stories—comic strips and little books." —YVETTE KAPLAN

mation in a roundabout way. From the time I was 12 until my early 20s I played music in a band. Then I went back and got my degree in advertising with an art minor.

Oddly enough, after I moved down to Portland, I used to run by Will Vinton Studios, a company known for their claymation. They did the Domino Pizza Noid and the California Raisins. As I jogged by, I'd see the clay characters in the window, and knew I'd just love to work there. In another strange twist of fate, I ended up moving across the hall from a producer who worked there. I had done some sculptures when I was younger, so I showed her some of my work. She must have liked my work because she put me in touch with her art director and before I knew it I was hired to build models and props for stop-motion animation.

What was the first cartoon you ever drew in your career as an animator?

—Peter C., age 13

Yvette: When I got out of school, I animated on commercials but my first big break came when a friend of mine was directing a show for a brand-new cable network called Nickelodeon. The show was called *Doug*, and it was all hand-drawn. I loved it, and I did some really cute animation. I went from animation to being a director all based on a little bit of animation I did for an episode called "Doug Can't Dance." Doug was dancing with the love of his life, Patty Mayonnaise. He was so transfixed on her that he didn't know how to dance. He was

Yvette Kaplan

standing there flapping his hands, and Patty said to him, "Move your feet, move your feet." So I had Doug look down at his foot like he had never seen it before. He picked it up like it was this strange thing and moved it. I was directing, really. The producers liked what I did and hired me as a director.

Tom: The first thing I animated was an M&Ms mini commercial. I animated a red M&M. And I modeled the lips on a green M&M.

Did anyone you know ever tell you that being an animator wasn't a serious job? If so, how did you respond and feel?

–Sharleen C., age 13

Yvette: That's a great and very thoughtful question. I know that that has been a very real challenge for some of my fellow animators, especially if they have come from a family of professionals like doctors, lawyers, or financial or business people. But luckily, in my case, I always received lots of encouragement and support from my family, especially my father, who was a factory worker his whole life—someone who, for many reasons, had much more talent and potential than he ever lived up to. I believe that he had a dream for me and it was for me to spend my life doing something that I loved. Even when I was struggling, he never even suggested I find something else to pursue. I, like he, would encourage you to stick to your dreams, as long as you are willing to work hard for them.

Tom: Being an entertainer, like an animator, is a serious job. It's not a normal job, though. Working with animators is like being on the Island of Misfit Toys—we're all strange, but we all fit together. We don't think of ourselves as eccentric, but we are misfits compared to other jobs.

What are your biggest challenges?

—Ana Z., age 13

Yvette: The animator is an actor with a pencil, and the biggest challenge being in animation is being a good storyteller and caring about communicating to your audience. You have to respect your characters. My focus as an animation director is always about character and story.

Tom: The hardest thing is still to do the writing and have good characters. A lot of us who are artists want to jump the gun and work on the characters before we have a really good story to tell. First and foremost is a really great story, and so many animated films fall short. They start to look like a factory turned them out. Also, the software and technology is continually changing and you have to keep up with that. In computer animation, you need to keep learning about the process. Some computer animators specialize in just water and hair and they're highly sought after.

Where do you get your ideas from?

—Zach M., age 13

Yvette: I believe ideas come when least expected. Sometimes I wake up in the middle of the night with an inspiration for a particular project. Other times I am hit with an inspiration while walking in the street, or listening to music, or reading. The important thing is to act on them, to make them real. That is something I am always struggling with—the discipline to actually put those bursts of inspiration onto paper.

Tom: I think ideas generally come from real life. There are things that happen in real life that are crazier than fiction. I suggest to students that they be really observant—take a moment and watch how people walk and you will see the strangest walks. Use those.

Do you enjoy doing your job?

—Martha R., age 13

Yvette: Yes. After all the years in the industry, I can honestly say that no matter the roller coaster ups and downs, of which there are many, it has been a joy. I have been lucky enough to meet and work with wonderful, creative people and have been involved with some extremely enjoyable projects and characters. I love telling stories, I love creating characters and knowing that I have helped make an audience laugh or cry and have hopefully created something they will always remember.

Tom: I enjoy it. It's not that I choose to do it, I have to do it. I've always been driven by doing some form of art.

How many years does it take you to create and draw your characters?

−Juan L., age 13

Yvette: I have a very simple and fluid drawing style, a few lines and dots and there it is—I'd say it takes no more than five minutes! But the real work is in creating a life for that character—giving it personality and making it real. As for the actual animation process, it is definitely time-consuming. A typical short, about seven minutes long—typically takes about four months, and a 60-minute movie I directed recently took one year, and that's with a very large staff of animators!

Tom: I'm doing computer-generated imagery (CGI) on a small independent feature film now. This is the first long-sustained story I've done. This film will take 15–16 months for the animation schedule. We have to turn out three finished scenes of animation a week, and that's almost impossible to do.

How hard is it to animate things the way you imagine?

−Andres R., age 13

Yvette: With a team of great artists, writers, actors, and musicians that I have been lucky enough to work with, it hasn't been too hard at all. It just takes time and patience—and the bigger budgets a large studio offers! But when I have made my own short films in the past, I admit it has been much harder. I would see every little mistake, every imperfect drawing, every technical error. I had to learn not to be so hard on myself, to pat myself on the back for creating something that could communicate to others, even if it may have been slightly different in my mind. If you have that desire to make what is in your mind real, you will do whatever you need to do to achieve it— but don't ever negate the work you do on your way there. It is all part of it.

Tom Sorem

Tom: It can be really challenging. I have been presented many times throughout my career with things I have never done before. I was trying to animate a Hershey's Kiss and it was just not turning out the way I imagined. Sometimes it doesn't always work. CGI is great because you can play it back right away and see if you are capturing what is in your imagination. When you shoot on film, you have to send the film to processing and it could take days before you could review it.

CHAPTER 7

Virtual Apprentice

CARTOON ANIMATOR FOR A DAY

Early on, animation came out of studios, where many talented individuals worked as a team. Today, the Internet makes it possible for you to learn this art form on your own and to produce short animated films and even distribute them to an audience. So there's no reason to wait: Your career as an animator can begin today!

Here's a timeline of activities to try by yourself or with your friends, or you can turn your classroom into an animation studio:

8:00 2-D animators don't draw every frame from scratch—they trace over drawings to make sure characters are positioned and sized consistently. Get some tracing paper, a pencil, and some comic books. Choose a character and spend time tracing it in different poses. Focus on the main shapes (don't worry about the smaller details). Once you've spent some time tracing the character, try drawing it freehand, too.

9:00 Time for some "life drawing." Even computer animators benefit from practice drawing live models. Take turns using your classmates as models for your drawings, or find a mirror and sketch yourself. You don't have to just draw people—try your hand at sketching objects, too.

10:00 The most basic animation lesson is the Bouncing Ball. Master this, and you'll have experience with an essential animation technique called "squash and stretch." Go to http://www.awn.com/tooninstitute/les sonplan/bounceball.htm and watch the lesson, then animate your own ball. (Almost anyone can draw a rough circle, so be sure to try this even if you don't have any drawing experience.)

11:00 Expert animators can express emotions with just a line or two. Create an "emotional scrapbook" you can refer to when you are drawing: Browse through magazines and cut out pictures of faces that show different emotions. Study them closely to see how the muscles in each face move. Draw a simple face and then change the features to show six to eight different emotions. If you're working in class or with a friend, trade drawings and see if you can guess which emotions you're trying to express.

12:00 Time for lunch—and don't forget the carrots, doc!

1:00 Invent a character you would like to animate: Come up with a fun name, a voice, and a personality. If your drawing skills are shaky, team up with an artistic friend or classmate and work together on this project. One of you can dream up a great name and a kooky voice and personality; someone can draw the outlines, and someone else can fill in the color. Try to make each other laugh.

2:00 Draw your character in a series of poses that express his/her/its personality. Use a pencil and keep erasing until you're happy with your work.

3:00 Create a storyboard featuring your character in an action sequence. A storyboard is a lot like a comic book page that tells a story using a sequence of pictures. Draw each frame (these can be very rough sketches—most storyboards are) and then paste in order on a cardboard background.

4:00 Make a flipbook using a sketchpad. Working from back to front, draw a simple series of pictures in the upper right margin that will animate a simple action. Each picture should be slightly different from the preceding one. (If the pages are thin enough, you can trace over the drawing on the previous page, which creates a smoother effect.) Draw as many frames as you need to bring the action to life.

5:00 Aspiring animators collect all their best work in a portfolio. Assemble all the art you've created for these assignments, along with any other drawings you're especially proud of, in a folder. Then decorate the cover with your name and the character you created.

Virtual Apprentice
CARTOON ANIMATOR: FIELD REPORT

If this is your book, use the space below to jot down a few notes about your Virtual Apprentice experience (or use a blank sheet of paper if this book doesn't belong to you). What did you do? What did you learn? Which activities did you enjoy the most? Don't be stingy with the details?

8:00 COMIC BOOK SKETCHES: _____
_____
_____
_____

9:00 LIFE DRAWING: _____
_____
_____
_____

10:00 BOUNCING BALL MASTER: _____
_____
_____
_____

11:00 EMOTIONAL SCRAPBOOK: _____
_____
_____
_____

12:00 LUNCH: _____
_____
_____

1:00 CHARACTER INVENTION: _____
_____
_____
_____

2:00 CHARACTER SKETCHES: _____
_____
_____
_____

3:00 STORYBOARD: _____
_____
_____
_____

4:00 FLIPBOOK: _____
_____
_____
_____

5:00 PORTFOLIO: _____
_____
_____
_____

Count Me In (or Out)

WILL WE SEE YOU IN THE FUNNY PAGES?

Still feel drawn to an animation career? Record your answers to the questions below on a separate sheet and review them after you animate your first 'toon.

When I go to the movies, I ☐ always ☐ sometimes ☐ never want to see an animated feature.

When I watch TV, I ☐ am ☐ am not as interested in the commercials as I am in the program, especially when they have animated special effects.

I think movies like *Narnia* that blend animation and live-action are ☐ creepy ☐ cool because:

_____

_____

While I'm yakking on the phone with my friends, I ☐ always ☐ sometimes ☐ never doodle.

If I were a cartoon character, my name would be: _____

and I would be (list 3 personality traits) _____

_____

On Saturday mornings, my friends can usually find me:

☐ Down at the local skatepark practicing my kickflips.

☐ Snuggled deep under the bedcovers reading the latest Harry Potter book.

☐ Glued to the tube, watching my favorite animated shows.

☐ Practicing on my drum set in the basement.

- ❑ Blasting villains into hyperspace on my Xbox 360.

- ❑ In the kitchen, whipping up a batch of my special peanut butter French toast.

The cruise ship I'm sailing on springs a leak! Three things I would take with me into the lifeboat are:

- ❑ My iPod shuffle, a change of underwear, and a can opener.

- ❑ A pencil, paper, and a Three Musketeers bar.

- ❑ An eyepatch, a spyglass, and a baked potato.

- ❑ Pepper, salt, and a slingshot.

- ❑ A deck of Tarot cards, a handkerchief, and a scale model of the Chrysler Building.

I'm chasing after a ball and I run right off the edge of a steep cliff! Check out what happens next:

- ❑ I just turn around and walk across the air and back to solid ground. The rules of physics don't apply in MY crazy world!

- ❑ I fire up the jetpack that I always wear for these types of emergencies and enjoy a little bird's-eye tour of the countryside.

- ❑ I grab for a root that's sticking out of the dirt and manage to pull myself back up with a combination of brute strength and sheer adrenaline.

- ❑ I wake up screaming and find I've just fallen out of bed.

If I had an extra $100, I would:

- ❑ Bury it in an old pickle jar in the backyard.

- ❑ Buy the boxed set of *The Looney Tunes Golden Collection* on DVD.

- ❑ Give it to the bully who's always taking my lunch money.

- ❑ Invest it in a college fund. It's never too soon to start saving for med school!

- ❑ Rush right down to the mall and buy those shoes I've been drooling over.

- ❑ Spend it all on organic chocolate, of course!

- ❑ Donate it to the Naked Mole Rat Rescue Society.

APPENDIX

More Resources for Young Cartoon Animators

BOOKS

Hahn, Don. *Animation Magic*. New York: Disney Press, 2005.

Hart, Christopher. *Christopher Hart's Animation Studio*. New York: Watson-Guptill Publications, 2003.

Hart, Christopher. *How to Draw Animation*. New York: Watson-Guptill Publications, 1997.

Lockman, Darcy. *Computer Animation*. New York: Benchmark Books, 2000.

Thomas, Frank and Ollie Johnson. *The Illusion of Life: Disney Animation*. New York: Disney Editions, 1995.

PROFESSIONAL ASSOCIATIONS

International Animated Film Society
http://www.asifa-hollywood.org

Women in Animation
http://www.womeninanimation.org

WEB SITES

Animation Station
http://www.amazing-kids.org/anistation1.htm

The Annual Annie Awards Database
http://www.annieawards.org

The Big Cartoon Database
http://www.bcdb.com

Don Bluth's Animation Academy
http://www.donbluth.com/academy.html

DreamWorks Animation SKG
http://www.dreamworksanimation.com

Pixar
http://www.pixar.com

The Walt Disney Company
http://disney.go.com

INDEX